Black Boy Blues

Chris E. James

Chris E. James

ISBN: 1547253150
ISBN-13: 978-1547253159

DEDICATION

I wrote this book first and foremost for me. I needed to get all these
thoughts out of my head so they could in turn stop weighing so heavy on
my heart. Writing and sharing this collection of poetry is apart of my
healing and growing process. I am also sharing these poems because I am
confident someone else needs to hear them so they too can begin
to heal and grow.
I owe my growth to many special humans in my life.
Ron Mc and Stacey McAdoo for being willing to invest in me.
A.P.O.L.L.O. aka Marquese McFerguson for living a life of selflessness and
reminding me that my work is not in vain.
Tru McCoy for being a great brother and rocking with me even through our
arguments and disagreements.
Pilar Murphy, my 7th grade science teacher, for encouraging me to continue
writing even though I was doing it during her class.
My big brothers, Roderick McCoy and Jimmy McCoy, who I love dearly and
the major reasons why I grind so hard daily.
My mother, Sharon Hardaway, my first love who always believes in me and
is rooting for me even when she aint able to come to a show. I love you
Mama because you are the rock I know I'll forever be able to lean on.
Sandrekkia Morning, the woman that rocked with me for five looooong
years even when I was taking you through hell. I thank you because in 2012
when we met I thought I was doing something already. You reminded me
that I could go so much further. Thank you for believing in me.
Shout out out to all my children and all my nieces.
Thank you to all the supporters of my journey and everyone who has ever
came to The House of Art.
Thanks for stepping into my journey.
Enjoy these poems.

Chris E. James

CONTENTS

Chris E. James

Black Boy Blues

FOREWORD

Chris James is a poet and educator who has spent the last decade changing the artist landscape of the Greater Little Rock Community. He is not only an award winning and accomplished artist that has performed across the United States, he has also worked tirelessly to create and implement artistic programming in academic institutions that inspires students and equips teachers with the skills to tap into their student's full artistic potential. To his credit, Mr. James has also created innovative programs that combine the arts with economic development and entrepreneurship.

Most people view the word creative as an adjective. They consider it a word that describes the things a person does. However, when it comes to Chris, creative is not only an adjective that describes the work he does, it is a noun, because it describes who he is as a person. His vision and ability to create artistic programming is only surpassed by his passion to change and impact the lives of young people. Mr. James has made an undeniable impact on the Greater Little Rock community and the state of Arkansas. It is an impact that will be felt for years to come. Mr. James is a quintessential artist and educator who views life through the frames of possibilities, rather than the lenses of limitation. He is an individual who works tirelessly to transform his dreams into realities. Simply put, Mr. James is a creative.

-Marquese L. McFerguson aka A.P.O.L.L.O.,
Professor at University of South Florida
PhD Student
Founder of Art Can Change the World

Hello, Reader! My name is Drekkia, if you care.

To begin with, before ever engaging in a serious relationship with Chris James (the author) I remember writing in my notebook about how I felt like I was supposed to be in his life for a reason. I felt drawn to him. The need for love and completeness radiating from his temple. I wanted to give that to him. To make him feel whole and beautiful. Me, an 18 year old with wisdom that didn't match my age. Nobody told me that there was just some things inside a man that stay broken and no matter what, I'd never be able to heal it. Who was I to think I had that kind of power anyway? Or maybe my perception of him was off? Doesn't matter anymore. Our "forever" lasted 4 years- more off than on.

When we first started to hang out, he had a newspaper he started called "The Essence of Blackness". Sometimes I would help him sell them for $1 each in store parking lots, proof read and even write articles. Once making it official during my first semester of college, I spent most of my time with him. Every Sunday for his weekly open mic and every weekend he'd make that 30 minute drive to pick me up from school (I do mean EVERY weekend). He was consistent. I would stay with him at his place. Then it went to sleeping on an air mattress at his moms house. We rode in the freezing cold without heat for months, in that old Expedition he loved. We even worked together. So, as you can see we were close and had a chance to experience many phases of life together. It's a wonder why we didn't make it. Why am I now his ex fiancée, writing a foreword for his newest book? Strange. But he's always made me feel included in his endeavors and like my voice mattered to him. Sounds like "hashtag RelationshipGoals" huh? Maybe. He gave me the best/worse four years of my life. I think he may even discuss the details on that in this book but you have to read it to find out.

Any who, on a more serious note, as I sit here writing this I'm honored. Chris is one of the most talented writers I know. He writes with ease and Heaven-sent purpose. Chris has always been a star in my eyes. One that I admire and have learned so much from.

He has such a powerful story to tell. To still be alive and pushing through the adversity he faced growing up- from poverty, losing his brothers to the system and having to practically guide himself through this life. I can't wrap my mind around how he beat the odds. I never told him but he truly is one that's been chosen by God. He possesses a kind of strength that can only be God given! He overcame the kind of struggles that crush the weak, make some commit suicide and lead others to drugs. He's one of much endurance and passion. Consistency, pain, confusion and determination.

My love. My baby. So strong and full greatness. Unmatched in his talent and work ethic. He is worthy of much praise. I know you will enjoy his work on more levels than one.

My Why?

I was asked
"Out of all the things you could've done with your life,
why did you choose to do poetry?"
I tell em' because
I got somethin to say.
Somethin that may add some day to your dark
some light to your night.
Somethin that may change your thoughts of suicide to
thoughts of life
make you wanna reincarnate your wrongs to rights.
I got somethin to say that may make a black boy believe
in his dreams when it seems the odds against him are
impossible to beat.
I do it because of that one time'
when the older white man rolled up to me in a
wheelchair after a show.
He told me he aint been able to hear in over 20 years

without his hearing aid but that night without it
he was able to hear every word that I spoke.
I do it because I guess I'm niece and believe I can
change a life.
I heard that words have power
I am trying to transform my metaphors into hands
and reach
a lost soul.
Pull em out of that dark hole and show em that it's better
on the other side.
I do it because my brothers are in the hole
in a correctional facility.
And lately, they don't dream no more
More consumed with night mares.
I do it because somebody other than me believes in me
and needs me
to win.

BLACK BOY, WRITE

WHO AM I?

Who am I?

Well I'm a boy;

a product of an absent father since 1990

I'm still trying to find em.

I think he's somewhere hiding in the hallways of my youth and

I'm waiting for him to appear like a magic trick.

While I'm waiting impatient I do a lot of studying, reading,

researching, experimenting and failing while learning to be a man.

I don't wanna be that boy no more.

I aint got too much pride to admit that it's lot

I still don't understand.

I am a work of art in progress.

I was told in order to be a king Ima need me a Queen.

One that's loyal and supportive is what I'm seeking.

If you see her tell her I need her

to believe in me

to see what I sometimes don't see in me

to breath life in me and with that same breath

take the moon and sun and breath light in me

because somedays my days are dark.

I'm whole but I'm also a whole lot of broken pieces

pieced with

problems and hurt

held together by prayers and hope.

I've been through some things I aint yet found peace with.

I've learned that holding on can be the thing that hurt you most.

I'm learning to let go.

I'm working to forgive.

No longer hold back my tears

I often cry and watch rivers and oceans be formed from my eyes

In my own mind I've built a boat so I can float on those waters

during the many times suicide crossed my mind wanting to eliminate

the depression

acting as if God didn't build me strong enough

to handle the pressure.

Who am I?

I am 16 year old boy who lost both of his brothers

Don't visit them much. It hurt too much.

Feels like I'm reliving their funerals all over again each time I visit.

The jail cells and penitentiaries are their caskets and grave sites

the prison sentences the writing on their tombstones

Watched their dreams spiral down drains

as THEY traveled down pipelines to prisons

Products of poverty.

Mama did the best she could but how could she fly us from the

nest when struggle and America had them strings on her wings.

Minimum waged her dreams.

Told her to work two and three jobs

while the streets babysit her sons.

Raised them to be thugs.

Made them to believe that they didn't have no real home

and that with her would be only place they'd be loved.

I watched my brothers hold her hand and play

while I put on my headphones

and tried to ignore her seductive song.

She still seduced me. I was 16 with a son of my own.

Father was gone and mama was too busy, trying to feed me,

to tell me don't be out here acting grown.

Who am I?

Im a 27 year old boy/ man who feels alone

like Im out here trying to figure it out on my own.

Chasing a dream sometimes I don't believe is mine.

I'm afraid of my own self.

My thoughts and ideas ring like police sirens that won't stop.

Most days I wanna turn it all off and hide in the dark where

people cant't hear me scream.

This dream won't allow me to sleep in peace.

I'm afraid I won't succeed so I often jump in with both feet

willing to risk it all

even though it aint much.

I'm in a rush to get my piece of this pie I've been baking for a

while now.

Who am I?

I'm a wounded solider in love.

Suffering from wounds from previous wars

I mean relationships I've been in.

Diagnosed with PTSD

Can't help but to imagine the man between the legs of the woman

I once I loved

Who told me he was just a friend.

I hear her screaming his name, her nails in his back telling him
sweet hymns I thought were sacred for me.
Can't help but see her in every woman these days.
I carry trust issues like bullets in magazines
I shoot off insecurities in the direction of innocent bystanders
who have nothing to do with this war.
I often treat women trying to love me like enemies when they are
the very allies I need.
Who am I?
I'm the brother in the night trying to find his way to the light.
Been in this dark place too long.
I'm ready to go home.
I'm a man who don't wanna be that boy no more.
Ready to discard all this baggage
It's been weighing me down.
I'm ready to dust off these wings and fly high over my lows
I am finally ready to let go and go
so I can grow
to my full potential.
I'm taking control.
I accept the fact that life aint a destination but a process, a journey.
I'm embracing my journey.
Who am I?
Well I'm a poem that God
aint yet done writing.
Stay tuned.

WRITERS BLOCK

Lately I've been stuck and the wheels won't turn.

The lights won't come on and I've never been a fan of the dark

I scream and my echo bounces off the walls; No one hears me

I am dancing in the middle of traffic and the world just keeps

passing like I don't exist

It's so empty and lonely in here

My tongue now trapped in the basement of a hollow place

It's become so silent in here

I turn the knobs on the sink

but it seems the well of water has run dry

Call the phone of a friend but it just keeps on ringing

I go back to the bedroom and lie on my back in the bed and stare

at the ceiling as I sink in my fear of not knowing.

Try not think about tomorrow but yesterday is gone

and today won't let me stay any longer.

I ask time to let me borrow some

but he claims he's got none to give.

So I press snooze on the alarm because I'd much rather be sleep

At least then I could dream about the possibilities

of something better

But the alarm always wakes me back up

On these days, I wish I could clock out

Tired trying to figure it out

Why does life have to be so much like math?

And have a specific order of operations

to get this one mystery answer

Today, I want to get everything wrong

just to spite the concept of being right

I wanna drop everything and be free of everything

Cut all ties that noose my very being

No longer wanna be strange fruit on the popular trees of these

so called American Dreams

I just wanna be free

Run away from all the pain that stains my sanity

Can't let what I been through get the best of me

I know these trials and tribulations just testing me

Can't let the demons surrounding get the rest of me

I know it's a few angels out there somewhere

willing to invest in me

I just want some wings so I can take flight

Soar to moon and land amongst the stars

I mean I don't want much. Just enough to afford a smile

It's been a while now since I've last had the luxury

Life for me aint been no crystal stair; it's had tacks in it

and splinters

I often imagine Langston's mother is having this conversation

with me

"Boy don't you turn back. Don't you set down on the steps
Tellin me to keep climbin.
If you keep searching eventually you'll find it.
Eventually you find that you were never lost and finding yourself
was only a figment of the imagination.
Sometimes we gotta let go, lose ourselves in the things we love
most so you can find self in the palms of your passion.
Sometimes we gotta be a contradiction, accepting there is not
always truth in our answers or the fact that things evolve
and we must to.
Change, after all, is inevitable.
Aint no editing what God already penned in his notepad.
But I find myself giving this poem he's written a bad review.
Because I dislike the plot, aint no fan of this spot he got me in.
I don't wanna play this role. I don't see the purpose in any of it.
Then again maybe it just aint for me to understand.

My girl quotes a line from one of my old poems.
We laugh and reminisce.
She says, "Damn bae. You used to be the shit."
Then asks, "Why did you ever stop writing?"
I respond, "I guess I just ran out of things to say."

WRITING FOR ME

I don't know which day it was
but one day I stopped writing for me
and I started writing for you
for an applause
to entertain and persuade your thoughts of me.
One day I began to care
as if I needed your validation to matter.
I used to push pens with purpose
with the goal to serve you hope
Stand on blocks eager to share with any ear that was willing to
let my words enter.
I was a fiend for your fix.
I got high whenever your mind was blown and your heart was
stole by my passion.
I used to love this art called poetry.
She saved my life
when I was but a boy drowning in a sea of uncertainty.
She gave me wings when I could barely walk
Gave me a voice when my tongue was tied and mouth didn't
wanna open.
Til this day she holds my hand when I am in doubt.
Tells me to write and it'll be alright
She is the purest thing I know
I am ashamed for ever taking her presence for granted.
I owe you the world
because you gave me one.
So in the mean time I'll get back to writing
and hope my metaphors, similes, nouns and verbs are enough.

SCHOOL DAZE

I rode through my old neighborhood attempting to not forget
where I come from.
I saw much hadn't changed.
I suppose the struggle is hereditary.
Impossible to escape our parents circumstances.
Hand me down poverty.
It's crazy because not long ago we acted as if we were immune to
this reality. Talking about "mane that would never be me."
It's 7 years later, I see many of my classmates looking twice their
age mascaraed in pain, dressed in designer struggle.
You wear it so well.
Seems like a week ago we all planned to prevail,
overcome adversity, attend college Universities, come back and
sow seeds in the community.
I guess life got the best of us.
Under estimated the opponent and now many of us are down for
the count wishing we could rewind back to round 1 when before our
eyes were swollen shut and we had vision
before our bodies were worn and we were full of drive.
Should have listened. Now you're 25 riding bikes that only take
you 25 miles per hour.
Leave home a hour early to be at work on time.
We took time for granted. Now time done passed us up.
Procrastination finally caught up with us
and time can't be bought back.
Before I graduated high school into adulthood I wish someone
would have told me that life is about to get real real real fast.
Instead I endured life's blows without warning.
Hard times constantly stinging like bees swarming.
Babies and bills. Heartbreaks and headaches.
Regrets and disappointments.
The other day I went to my old neighborhood and saw my

elementary crush walking and cracked out.
I saw my old best friend too drunk and high to hold a
conversation or look me in my eyes.
I saw the guy all the boys wanted to be and all the girls used to
love, sitting at bus stop lonely like he was looking for love.
I drove to the gas station and saw the man I used to want to be
wearing make-up, high heels and a purse.
I'm not sure who was more confused, me or him.
I'm not sure who was more hurt, me or them.
Because none of us chose to be where we are.
I mean who aspires to be a crackhead or alive dead in the head,
stuck in these ghetto boondocks?
I suppose some were less fortunate than others.
I don't imagine prison was the paradise my brothers dreamed of.
I doubt being a mother with no King to crown her Queen was the
fairytale she'd been fantasizing about.
We all begin together on this climb.
It was not my plan to be on this mountain top alone.
Now a days I feel so alone
although I'm often surrounded by many.
I haven't went to visit my brothers in those in prisons in over 5
years. I blame them for my loneliness.
I often wish I was an artist and that my name was God
so I could recreate our circumstances.
I'd paint my mother a smile
I'd paint Keisha a husband, Jeremy a father,
I'd paint Adonis, Korey, Benard a life pass the age of 25
I'd paint my brothers back into my life.
But too bad I am just a man and
I can't turn back Gods' hands of time.
I rode through my old neighborhood the other day attempting to
not forget where I come from.
I saw much hadn't changed.

MY MAMA

"Oh Mama, I know act a fool.
Oh Mama, I even skipped some school.
Oh Mama, just to smoke some Kools.
Oh Mama, thank for the food.
Oh Mama, thank you for the whoopins.
Oh Mama,
I just wanna say
I love you"
This is a poem about my Mama
but first I'd like to point out the disturbing fact
that the rapper Lil Boosies' release from prison was celebrated
more than my mother was for raising three black boys to men.
I'm on my Kanye.
I'll let you have your moment but I think that was some straight
bull....
my mother has been making platinum meals out of koolaid and
syrup sandwiches way before a Lil Boosie
was making platinum records.
For the record
my mother was cutting me and my brothers Hi-lows in the kitchen
way before there was ever a thing called a Boosie fade.
True fact.
My Mama invented gangsta rap.
In the 80's she came out with tracks like
I'll beat yo butt if you don't clean yo room,
This is my House,
and my favorite track ever
Get yo Shit together in that school or go live with yo
Triflin Daddy.
I danced to the rhythm of her discipline.
I can testify that she lived by every rhyme.
None of this imitating false images like todays' rapper.
My Mama was the real deal.

When I was in the third grade, she whooped me in the school
bathroom with my own belt and made me walk back to class like
nothing even happened.
I remember the time my brother, Rod, told my Mama
"I'll wash the dishes when I get ready"(Hmmph)
She broke the broom on his back.
My Mama broke her back to give us the little that we had.
It's amazing how she made poverty feel like royalty
Roman noodles taste like Fettuccini alfredo
Disconnected lights look like romance nights the way we had
candles lit throughout the house.
We rocked Shaquille O'Neal tennis shoes like they were Jordans
with our Jordache jeans.
We made Starter look like Nike the way we had the socks to match
the shirt.
She couldn't afford to buy us FUBU but the BUFU from the
bootleg man was cool.
We were too fresh at school
No one could ever tell us nothin.
My mama taught me everything I know
How to change a bike tire
how to cut grass
how to put a worm on a hook
how to cook
how to shave and the best ways to save.
Now days, I bargain shop at Goodwill and Savers
instead of spending hundreds of dollars for the sake of a name
Ralph Lauren, Tommy Hilfiger, Nautica, Levi.
I don't know any of them anyway.
My mama never stepped foot in anyones college
but she was definitely a Doctor.
She had a remedy for every illness we ever contracted and an
answer for every problem we ever encountered.
My mother is Angela Davis, Shirley Chisolm, Maya Angelou,

Harriet Tubman, Sojourner Truth and Mary MeCloud Bethune
all wrapped in one.
She is every woman
Phenomenal she is.
She's been creating history since the genesis of time
but yet to be recognized for being more than the rib of a man.
She deserves a round of applause for taking on the role of a man
without once putting her hand out for a hand-out.
She's been fighting in this war called motherhood since her
adolescence.
She has the stress and stretch marks to prove it.
She's been bruised from battles but never has she been broken.
She burns beautiful like a bonfire blazing in the night.
Boy was her birth bountiful
Breath-taking like the site of butterflies and blossoms in the
beginning of spring.
I know my opinion of my mother may be biased but
she indisputably deserves to have her brilliance broadcasted on
billboards across the world.
So until that happens
I'll celebrate my Mama through my poems.

SOMETHIN' ABOUT A GIRL

Chris James

BEAUTY FOR SALE?

Society has lied to you and told you that…..
For a small price, you can be beautiful.
Going once! Going Twice!
Sold………..
to every woman who wants a man
and every young girl who wants to fit in.
The average woman in America spends at least $300-$500 a
month trying to maintain
medias' perception of what beauty is.
Somewhere, somehow something has gone terribly wrong.
Eight year old girls are getting pedicures and bikini waxes.
By age 15, they'll be saving their allowance for breast implants and
Nikki Minaj butt duplications.
The store by my house sales booty pads.
My twin daughters asked for Barbie dolls for their 3rd birthday.
I bought coloring books instead because I refuse to contribute to
the belief that a doll is the idea for what they should be striving to be.
Long straight hair but no brains.
Perfect smile but nothing of substance to say.
Large breast but no heart to love. Living life just to fit in
a box on a shelf waiting to be sold.
I asked a young lady why she spent so much time getting dressed
every day. She responded "because I like to feel beautiful."
I told her, beauty isn't something you just put on and take off like
a mask.
You were born with it.
There is no need for Maybelline to make believe something you
already are.
You are perfect on purpose, perfectly imperfect. You are worth it
because you are worthy. You are phenomenal. Maya Angelou told you
so in 1978. Chaka Khan sang you are every woman. India Arie told ya
you are not your hair, your nails or the skin you are in

And God has constantly reminded the world how magnificent you
already are since the beginning of time.
But somewhere down the line, you started trying
to be what took no effort in the first place.
Botox, lipo and anorexia will make you sexy but only in the eyes
of those hoping to behold your booty.
Striving to be fine as wine, he will drink you til he's drunk.
Working to become a dime, he'll spend you up and make change,
leaving you to be only a cent.
Personality piss poor but still expecting to marry a Idris Elba or
Robin Thicke
It doesn't make sense that you are God's most prized creation
but yet to realize that you are royalty.
Daughters of Cleopatra and Nefatima.
Put on your crown and don't dare take it off again.
Society has bamboozled you.
Has taken your image, reconstructed it's essence, put it in a bottle
and convinced you to buy it
over and over again.
Men, our women have been brainwashed.
Don't try to save them.
It's already too late but we can still save our daughters.
Go home and tell them repeatedly that
beauty isn't something you can buy.
You were born with it.
Women, beauty isn't something you can buy.
You were born with it.
You don't have put on pounds of make-up
or be a size zero to be beautiful.
You don't have to put on tall heals and expensive or little to no
clothes to be sexy.
Beauty is in your heart.
Sexy is in YOUR confidence.
Go home and grab all your receipts and all the things that you

were convinced to believe makes you beautiful.
Pack them in the biggest bags you own
go back to the retailer and tell em
"I NEED – A – REFUND."

U G L Y

U G L Y, you aint got no alibi.
You ugly.
Yeah yeah you UGLY.
Unpleasant, repulsive, unappealing, unlovely, obnoxious, awful,
repugnant, vile, foul, monstrous, flat out unacceptable.
UGLY.
You got the perfect body and your facial features are flawless
so to be clear I'on mean it in a physical sense but emotionally
mentally and especially when it comes down to your personality
you're ugly.
Your character is quite cynical.
Always somehow land your opinions in the center of negativity.
Don't see the good in nothing or nobody.
You are by the far the biggest pessimist to ever exist.
Always got something bad to say.
Never in my days of knowing you have I heard genuine
compliments fall from your lips.
You always fashion and beauty police
Quick to rate and judge everyone else's appearance before you've
even considered looking in your own mirror.
Who died and made you the God of societies standards?
You should get your own toilet tissue since you the shit.
You should be a travel agent because you a trip.
I hope and pray you don't trip and fall on your face
because I imagine all that negative energy you carry around can
weigh you down.
Is it possible to turn your frown upside down?
I mean smiling every now and again aint never hurt nobody.
Even Ice Cube had Good day.
My ancestors were beaten, raped, tortured as slaves and shackled
in chains but I'm sure there were days when even they smiled and

found beauty in the people around them.

Yo!

You do realize the people closest to you

are beginning to unlove you.

They are beginning realize it's not just something you do for

laughs but it's actually who you are.

You're consumed by your ugly behaviors.

You wear them as if they are louis vuitton or Michael Kors

apparel and accessories.

You've become so accustom to finding pleasure in the humiliation

of others it's become a necessity and that is why you are so UGLY.

Please don't for a moment think I am sharing these things to make

you feel insecure or to get under your skin.

Think of this as an intervention, a cry for you to change.

I understand that maybe you were hurt once upon a time.

But don't you think it's time you start searching for

your happily ever after.

I mean Regina did. Even Mr.Gold until....

well we know what with him.

But if you don't change now, your grandchildren will complain

about coming to visit you.

Your children will argue about who will say the eulogy because no

one wants to speak on your behalf because no one will have anything

nice to say because you never did.

Oh! and you'll be lonely with a lot of cats.

U G L Y

You aint got no alibi

because there absolutely no reason anyone should be that UGLY.

DON'T FIT IN

My daughter, Rhyleigh, says to me
"Daddy I don't wanna go to school anymore because the other
kids laugh at me and say I got a light bulb head."
So I told her
Don't allow their tainted tongues to tremble
or trouble your throne
because remember, you are a Queen
so don't ever attempt to metamorph into metaphors
and compare yourself to people or things that you aren't like
because you are a
CIRCLE
well rounded, 360 degrees of perfection
and societies perception of what beauty is
will attempt to anorex your self-esteem
until it's nothing of you left.
Maybelline will attempt to make you believe
that you need make up to cover the girl you are
to become a woman of worth.
And boys will attempt to use your beauty as target practice
aiming to convince their peers and themselves that they are
the men that they have yet to learn how to be.
So keep your eye on their bull.
I
just need You
to be prepared
Because when you are in positions of power
peasants will always be on the prowl for your place
but remind them that you are irreplaceable.
Stand your ground.
Don't be moved by their bulldozers of bitterness
attempting to twin tower collapse your confidence.

Use their sticks and stones as stepping stones
for your stairway to success.
Shine bright like a diamond.
Yes, you are the hardest and most precious substance on Earth
but you are still as soft as sunny sunday mornings.
It's alright to allow tears to leak from the windows to your soul.
Cry yourself a river
but always remember to smile
because your smile
takes fresh breaths of air from lungs
and resuscitates life into loss and lifeless souls.
You give birth to better days
just by simply waking up in the morning.
You are important and you already matter
just as much as matter
and oxygen and carbon dioxide and the ozone.
You are a pot of gold.
Your thoughts are winning lottery tickets.
Your mind is worth millions
so don't ever waist your time
I mean your money
I mean your mind
worrying about those other kids
because remember,
you are a Queen
so there is never a need to metamorph into metaphors and
compare yourself to people or things you aren't like
because you are a CIRCLE
well rounded, 360 degrees of perfection.
You will never fit in
so get used to standing out.

TEACH EM EARLY

The other day my daughter, Chrissette, tells me a boy in her
kindergarten class keeps hitting her.
I asked if she told the teacher.
She says Yes but the teacher tells her not to tattle tale.
So I tell my daughter if a boy or girl ever puts their hands on you
or says something that makes you feel uncomfortable you raise
your hand and you tattle tale.
If you are ignored, stand up
lift your tongue and roar like lion.
Speak up until you are acknowledged
because aint no such thing as being silent
especially when you're being bothered.
If they got a problem tell em you got a father that 5'7
but more like 7'5 when it comes to protecting his daughters.
Remind em that you descendants of Africans
and being silent aint apart of your culture.
It's in your DNA to make noise.
I'll be damned if any of my daughters grow up to think
they aint got a voice or a choice
Especially if some man ever decide he can use his hands
to go upside your head
or to use his lies and persuasiveness to get inside your head or
between your legs
Abuse your heart, pull your emotions like strings on a puppet.
You aint gone never be nobody's puppet.
Let them big head boys know that your daddy be taking trips
every other summer to the moon just to show he love you
and if they aint trying to do the same then "remove em".
Remove them from your presence.
Let em know they aint worthy of your gifts.
If they get mad tell em that's fine

but ya bets keep ya hands in ya pockets or come Monday morning
they won't have none.
Let em know it aint none of that grabbing and snatching
then laughing and later on apologizing about the matter.
Make sure he knows your body is a temple and it aint to be tainted
or tampered with.
Love is what love does
And love don't bloody lips, black eyes or bruise precious skin
Love don't call you bitch, say you aint shit until you feel like it
Love don't tell you lies, look you in your eyes, break your heart
and leave you in the dark to pick up the pieces.
Love touch you soft and hold you tight like locks
but leave you with a key if you ever need to leave.
Love don't hold you hostage against your will.
Love be the softest place on earth
Love make you weak in the knees like SWV
Love is free. Don't cost you a thing.
Just because he buy you nice things
don't mean you owe him a thing.
Don't ever let him convince you that he's the only thing you need
Without him you can't breath…
Baby know with or without a man you are already whole.
Although to be a wife is your goal you won't settle for the bare
minimum
because you are a maximum woman.
Don't ever settle for less
because you are the most
any man could ever wish for.
Chrisette, Chassity, Rhyleigh, Taliyah, Ronisha and NaNa
if I haven't told you lately,
I LOVE YOU.

COLDEST DAY IN HISTORY

Each year, over 4,000 women lose their lives because someone
didn't learn how to love them without using their hands.
27 year old Anita Brooks was shot and killed by her husband in
an apartment near 35th and Highland on Milwaukee's west side
around 1am Sunday morning.
Police confirmed that the incident
was a result of domestic violence.
And for that very reason, January 27th, 2013 was the coldest day
in Earth's history.
It was the first time the sun decided not to rise.
He was off mourning that Sunday morning
with the rest of the world.
Flowers that once blossomed in beauty lied limp and lifeless
like hunched backs with scoliosis.
That day, all bodies of water stood still like the wind did.
All birds, butterflies and bees tucked their wings for there was
no longer a reason to fly.
The Queen Bee had been robbed of her last breath.
Once word reached the core of the universe, the ground began
to rumble like hurricane Katrina was running from Ike.
All the trees ruffled their leaves
as if they were screaming to God
"What happened to our Queen? You were supposed to protect
her."
And God turned his back as tears began to burst from behind his
eyes like broken levees in New Orleans and thunder and lightning

roared from the clouds like never before as the sky began to cry
showers of rain for hours.

The world began flooding for a second time in history but God
issued no instructions for Noah to build an Ark this time.

The Queen had been robbed of her last breath.

No mercy was to be shown this time.

They say the man who had her heart loved her too much. Loved
her too much. Love her so much that he couldn't stop putting his
hands on her.

Reconstructing her beauty like he was a make-up artist covering
up this colored cover girl with black eyes and blue bruises.

Love aint supposed to hurt like this.

Like funeral services at 10:00am at All Saints Catholic Church.
3 year old daughter not knowing or understanding why her mama
is lying in a black box in front of the church or why her daddy
gotta spend the rest of his life behind bars because he couldn't
realize what her mama was worth.

R.I.P. and Gone But Not Forgotten airbrushed on shirts.

Roses broken from their bushes just to be placed on top of dirt.

I guess he took until death do us part too literal.

Now death is literally the epitome of her distance from us.

Love aint supposed to hurt like this.

All she ever wanted was to be a poet and a mother.

I still remember her baby girl crying in the audience
cheering her on.

She stood 5 feet, 5 inches short but had the voice of a giant.

She was a Queen and the stage was her thrown and the
microphone was her crown. She rocked it proudly as she stood on
stage slanging words, verbs and metaphors like street hustla's do
herb. I was a loyal customer. She had that blue magic.

It was magic the way she made words sound like songs being
sung by hummingbirds in the summertime.
I knew she was an angel the entire time because she had the
confidence and swag of a Goddess.
It's a shame y'all never got to meet her before her husband beat
her I mean loved her too much. They say he loved her too much.
They say he loved her so much that he couldn't stop putting
his hands on her.
Love aint supposed to hurt like this.
The Shirells used to sing "Mama said there'd be days like this.
Mama said there'd be days like this."
But I imagined her mama never told her
there'd be days like this
when his fist would kiss her lips and fracture her ribs.
They say he loved her too much. They say he loved her so
much that he couldn't stop putting
his hands on her.
27 year old Anita Brooks was shot and killed by her husband in
an apartment near 35th and Highland on Milwaukee's west side
around 1am Sunday morning. Police confirmed that the incident
was a result of domestic violence.
And for that very reason, January 27th, 2013 was the coldest
day in Earth's history.
It was the first time the sun decided not to rise.

Chris James

BLACK BOY MEETS LOVE

CRAZY LOVE

For the woman I can't help but love.
I hate you
so much
that if I saw you standing onside a road
I would ride right pass you
Only to turn around and offer you a ride home.
Our love is a contradiction
an oxymoron.
Bitter like the taste of dirt of tongue but sweet like apples with
caramel and cider on the side.
When we first met
she told me I was the definition of an asshole
then turned around and gave me her phone number.
I knew from the beginning
this relationship was going to be a roller coaster ride
going up and down
never sure of our direction.
We were just along for the ride.
Whenever the ride seemed to be over
we always got back in line
willing to do it all over again.
We were as a complicated as trigonometry
but we never dropped the class.
We just took our F and tried again next semester
even though packing our bags
and moving to Belair was an easier option.
We were at war in love.
We often shot each others emotions with words that pierced our
souls like hollow points
but always ended up nursing each others wounds with apologies.
We made no since like Bobby and Whitney

but made hits like Ike and Tina.
We often had heavy arguments like Jody and Yvette
but they always ended in love making and back scratching.
It's amazing how "I hate you" can turn to "I love you"
in the blink of an eye
in the change of a scene
in a matter of moments.
I remember the time she put her fist through the face of my
laptop because I went out without consulting with her.
I responded by putting my foot through the mirrors of her car.
We cuddled on the couch
the next day like nothing even happened.
This love thing is crazy.
I remember the time
she grabbed me by my shirt collar and said
"The only way out of this relationship is DEATH"
And she meant it.
I can't say I was bothered by her threat
because I'm not afraid of the concept of dying.
I am more afraid of living

without her.
It's something about her absence that leaves my heart with a hole.
It's something about her existence that makes me whole.
I can't quite put my finger on what it is but she has a hold on my
mind, body and soul.
This is
a Love Jones
a Darius and Nina kind of love.
I be the blues in her right thigh
trying to become the funk in her left.
This is a poem for a woman I can't help but love.
I call this
a blues for my future wife.

HOME

A roof
with four walls
Carpeted floors
chandeliers
windows
a front porch
living room with a couch
television and candles
Kitchen with fridge filled with just enough.
Breakfast, lunch and dinner
Bedroom
where sleep was commenced.

A familiar smell
Like comfort
Safe
No worries
Home.

She was my home
I lie on her chest for comfort
She would listen and reply honest.
She would tell me she loves me on repeat just in case I needed to
hear it.
I always needed to hear it.
Kept me warm when it was winter.
Most times it was winter.
I was imperfect
She accepted my flaws
even though it hurt her.
She knew I was hurting.
She would try to fix my brokenness

But somedays it seemed too severe
My pain would strike fires
burning my home
I was so destructive
Destroying the only thing truly good for me.
Eventually she rebuilt on the other side of town.
I am without my Home now.

HOME- LESS

She don't love me no more.

She say I pissed away what we had with last night's liquor

So I..... po up/ Drink

only to wake up and find her absent as a result of my actions.

Why niggas gotta realize what they had when it's gone?

Like the day when its night

Like the sun when it rain

Like sight when you're blind

Especially when it was so precious the entire time.

I wish I could put the days on rewind and rewind back to a time

before I made tears fall from her eyes.

I wish my apologies still mattered enough for her to stay after

my mistakes.

She said my sorries hold as much weight as loose feathers.

Promises of forever whisper in the whirling winds while I

Stevie wonder who's holding the keys to her heart.

She changed the locks and denied me access to her most

valuable organ.

The sound of organs with no keys

or strings to execute the sound it mellows.

Incomplete waves traveling through time.

Broken records playing on repeat like the sounds of black souls

burning in Mississippi.

Nights like this I wish rain drops would fall and put out the fire

I'm burning from the lack of my confessions.

Guess my skeletons wouldn't have hurt as much coming from

my mouth but instead you found out from the daily news.

My deceit on the front cover of your friends conversations.
You invested your trust, your stocks and bonds and got no return on your investment.
Damn!
All you wanted was a lifetime commitment
7 kids and a friendship.
But I treated it as if it was too much to ask for.
Now I'm lonely looking at my phone screen waiting for your name and number to appear in my text message notifications.
It's been 2,167 days and I'm still waiting
while I Stevie Wonder who's holding the key to your heart.
Because you still got mine.

RED RIBBONS

News just in. Your life will no longer normal again.
Your impressive number of one night stands and unprotected
sex with random women have earned you a prize you're sure to
NEVER get rid of.
The prize comes with a lifetime supply of meds, shortness of
breath, weight loss and DEATH.
Yes, DEATH.
And you won't be living as long as you probably expected.
Sorry to tell you but allowing your erections to control your
brain is the blame.
As of January 23rd, 2015 you are HIV positive.
Don't be surprised.
You did everything you
WEREN'T supposed to do
Like, making love to women you didn't know
well enough to love
Like always taking off the condom so you can get the full
feeling of her insides
Like being absent minded of status.
Telling yourself
It look good so it must be.
Now, the consequences are yours to keep
hold and cherish for the rest of your days.
Days aren't what they used to be.
They lack light like the darkness swallowed the sun
eternal eclipse in your eyes.
You're burning with anger like fire.

Hoping and waiting for someone to put it out.

Can I ask

Why are you mad?

It's your fault

Portraying the characteristics of a dog in heat

Humping every pooch with a cooch like

your life depended on it.

Like a squirrel you chased after those nuts;

acorns, pecans, pistacchios, almonds, cashews.

You didn't discriminate.

Talking about

The more the merrier.

You should've left those whores alone and married her.

Instead, you embarrassed her

Gave her a std and abandoned her.

You should have listened to me. I told you a thousand times

she was too good for you.

But noooooooo,

you just had to have your way

like she was an item on the McDonalds' menu.

You loved to pick those fast meals from the menu

when you had full course meals and a kitchen at home.

Key word, Home.

You had a Home.

Now you just a man with a leaking roof.

....

....

....

....

....

....

These are the conversations I often have with myself.
Conversations with the man in the mirror
My daily reminder that I'm dying a little bit more when the sun
and moon trade places on the faces of the Earth.
I don't smile like I used to.
I take each moment with a grain of salt.
Everything is half empty
Even me.
I am nostril deep in my tears
I've become accustom to the concept of drowning
But I've learned to pull myself up right before my last breath
leaks from lungs.
I don't know which is worse
Being ready to die or being terrified to live
It's crazy because I've always wanted to write an HIV poem
but I never imagined I'd be writing it in first person.

TEARS AND CHAINS

AMERICA LOVE STORY

"Oh say can you see by the dawn's early light,
What so proudly we hailed at the twilights last gleaming,
Whose broad stripes and bright stars.........."
I almost married her.
Our wedding colors were going to be red, white and blue.
Her dress draped in stars. My tuxedo was going army fatigues,
my rifle and helmet so I'd be ready to be at war in love.
Lady liberty was going to be her brides mate.
Uncle Sam my best man.
It was all planned. I was ready to pledge to her allegiance for the
rest of my life.
I even sang her songs while my right hand rested over my heart as
stars spangled like fireworks on the 4th of July.
What we had was beautiful.
We wore his and her shirts, her face imprinted on my chest like it
was my patriotic duty to claim her. I stood on front lines defending
her honor, willing to sacrifice my life for her name.
I showed her off to my friends like she was a trophy while they
turned their noses up at the ideal of our forever.
I thought to myself, "Oh they're just jealous" but they knew more
about her than I did.
Rumor has it, she wasn't as pure as I had been led to believe.
I thought we had a two way love affair.
Only to find out I was traveling on a one way street
to a dead end destination.
Why did you lie? Told me you loved me knowing you don't.
I guess you took pride in deceiving
watching me lie in this pool of love bleeding.
I can't believe I was in love with a monster.
What kind of mama allow her children to run around in white
sheets and hoods destroying families and neighborhoods?
It was you who commenced the purge on innocent people.

Cremated 4 little girls inside the church building
I bet you enjoyed them screaming
Dumped Emitts' youthful body in the river and watched him
sink,I bet you enjoyed him drowning
Lynched women and men in trees, executed boys and babies in
inner-city streets and refused to look at the damage you caused.
Denied every murder you committed even with the blood
decorated and drenched on your hands.
Then have the nerve to try and justify injustice.
And for the longest I've turned the other cheek refusing to believe
your true colors but even your neighbors and allies see your flaws.
I'd have to be a fool to ignore your sharp blade anticipating the
penetration of my back.
Oh how I wish I could take all the "I love you's" back.
Lady America, I don't love you no more
and quite frankly, I don't think I ever will again.
Because love aint supposed to hurt..... LIKE THIS!

MASS INCARCERATION

I heard a teacher say "We can't save them all. It'll be okay."
Then the preacher say "Save who you can and for the rest we'll
pray."
Parents say "I brought in the world and put clothes on they back
everyday."
America say "Good job folks. We'll take em. Put em in cages and
feed em three times a day."
From the cradle to the prison pipeline
They won't yo babies in cages.
America has implemented mass incarceration.
Since 1980 the state of California has built 22 prisons
and 1college university.
On average the state is paid thirty thousand taxpayer dollars
per inmate.
Meanwhile, I only get a $1,000 tax credit per child
And earn a salary not far from minimum wage for educating the
youth supposedly serving as our tomorrow.
I'm pissed.
Because obviously America believes the captivity of human bodies
is more beneficial than the nurturing of million dollar minds.
Meanwhile, the struggle has set up shop in the ghetto standing on
street corners like newsstands handing out crime
Headline in bold print advertise demise.
Struggle be holding presentations presenting drug sales, robbery
and violence as a way to suppress hard times
Music and Media come right behind and tell more lies.
Tell black kids to cook that dope, be a promiscuous hoe, be an
athlete or a rapper.
Other than that you aint got no hope.
So the youth put on their orange suits, I mean uniforms and fall in

line on the right side of the hallway in a single file line.
The students are in training to be inmates and teachers are the
prison guards.
No longer Jessica, Jerome, Phelisia or Elroy but inmate 17695
and 1387.
When the youth express their creative selves, they're told they are
breaking the rules and forced into a hole
with maximum insecurity.
Taught not shine so they dim their brightness and turn off their
light bulbs.
School system clips their wings of creativity
and then tell them the limit is the sky.
All while politicians and millionaires plan for their arrival by fixing
the overcrowding of jails by building more prisons rather than lessen
an inmate's times.
Like it aint already enough plantations in place.
"Tyrone for 10 years. Roderick for 25 years. Keisha for 15 years."
Place your bets on the babies because the prison system is a multi-
million dollar business on the stock market
and wall street is having a ball.
Leaving your children behind is the very key to gaining a return
on their investment.
And if you aint watering the seeds for these students to spring
into scholars you aint no different from those
who violently victimize their visions
Burglarize them of their dreams. Rape them of their imaginations.
You are literally standing on the sideline watching
their innocence be stolen.
Our youth are nailed to systematic walls like crosses
bleeding out potential like Jesus.
They are being sacrificed like lambs and their blood is drenched in
the palm of our hands. They are a drowning in the depth of societies
wading waters and on bended knees they have their arms stretched
out reaching for us to save them.

Reality is,
every child might not make it.
Question is, what are you going to do to save them?
They say they minds don't matter.
They'd rather put em on blocks and auction off they bodies.
From the cradle to the prison pipeline
They won't yo babies in cages.
America is on the prowl to recruit your child for mass
incarceration.

CAGED BIRD

"Do you know why the caged bird sings?
Do you know why the caged bird sings?
I know why the caged bird sings."
The caged bird sings because he can't see past the 25 years the
judge sentenced him 9 years ago.
The caged bird sings because he can't imagine his 2 daughters
being raised without him.
He can only see them growing up to be just like their mother
15 with first child
16 with second, high school drop-out
18 with third child
20 with fourth child premature
21 with fifth child
tubes still not tied
decided to become a lesbian so she can play catch up
with her friends
She felt she never had a childhood
she grew up too fast.
The caged bird sings because he now knows that his friends were
never friends for they never come to see him
and his family considers it a burden to drive two and three hours
to visit him in his new home
Prison.
He lies on his used pissed stained 4 inch mattress
in his 6x10 cell block
and the mattress seems to get more thin by the wake up
the walls close in closer by the awakening from a night mare
He says the meals have become so bitter that
he no longer tastes them
He just chews and swallows.
The caged bird sings

because his tears won't shed
so he sings them on the prison walls with a shank he made out of
scrap metal.
These walls are his canvas and his journal.
He sings because every day is constant reminder of life regrets
made mistakes
having to look over his shoulder
the same three bitter meals and
disappointments when a letter don't come today or the next day
or even the day after.
The caged bird sings because he knows his mother is struggling
and little brother is stuck between going to school and hustlin'.
The caged bird sings because his little brother for some reason
aint wrote or came see him in 6 years.

The caged bird is my brother.
The other day he wrote me a letter
asked me to send some pictures.
Said that's how they tell stories in there.
The letter read *I know you don't owe me anything but you my only lil
brother and you don't even write or come to see me. P.S. Family is all we got!*
The caged bird is my brother and the caged bird
could be your brother
your sister, your mother, your father and the caged bird
could very well be you.
So when they sing or cry
be sure to hear them.
They just wanna know that they're not forgotten.

PRISONER (TOO)

I have never been confined inside those walls
Had to spend days, weeks, months, years there.
Not been convicted of such a crime
to strip me of my freedom.
I don't know what it feels like to sleep on those beds
and box springs
that cause you back pains.
I've never had to sleep next to where I defecate.
I don't know what it feels like to miss your family
Anticipating their visits on Sundays at 11am
Nor how much it hurts when they don't or can't come.
I don't know how it feels to have to watch your children grow up
by staring at the pictures of them you've hung on those walls
over the years.
I don't know how it feels to have to watch over my back daily
to be surrounded by people who feel they have nothing to live for
to miss the touch of a woman
to try to remember.
I don't know what its feels like to be labeled a number
Inmates 138725 and 139398.
I don't know your pain.
But since 2006 when America snatched you from me
I too have been a prisoner.
I've created these walls
but somehow depression still got in.
I have bags beneath my eyes
from all the nights I couldn't sleep
afraid that you might've been harmed.
It's been 11 years but I still cry at least once a week
I'm expected to be the strong one

but I feel so weak without my two big brothers
around to protect me.
When I was a kid I thought I was invincible
because I knew you were never too far.
Now, you seem so far.
I want to hug you. Tell you "I love you."
I don't visit much because it hurts too much to see my heroes
defeated.
I've tried to write you letters but the pen won't stop shaking.
I can't keep the pages dry.
The tears are rivers that won't stop flowing.
I am still not sure how to deal with your absence.
It's a constant struggle.
I wish we could break the chains off.
I just want to break the chains off.
We are all prisoners
Just in different prisons.

BLACK MEN CRY

I'd like to speak to all the women
on behalf of every black man.
Today, I'd like to be totally honest.
I have no emotional capacity for your sorrows or your situations.
I have too much of my own baggage to borrow your burdens
and baby believe
usually I'd be willing to swallow my pride to pamper
and pacify your problems
but today, my sun rised on a different side of the mountain.
Yes, you still matter
but today I matter a little bit more.
I need you to hear me for once.
I've wiped your tears for years.
Today, I need you to wipe mine.
No, I was never forcefully penetrated
but I too have had my innocence stolen way before I knew what
it meant to be black and a man in America.
I've been touched and molested in ways words can't describe.
I've been in a war since the day I was born. Still trying to figure
out how being something so beautiful can be a burden?
It burns to know my life is a lottery ticket and at any given
moment, I could become some officers paid vacation.
The world's next hashtag, face on a t-shirt, news headline
excuse for a riot
some lawyers rise to fame.
I am just as much a man as any man but I too cry rivers.
Enough to fill the Nile. They have been running for a while now.
No it aint 1855 but I've been whipped by the world too many
times to keep count and my back is bout exhausted from bleeding
from these lashes.
It's easy for you to say suck it up. Be a man. Be a father.

But hell I aint seen neither in all my days, other than Uncle Phill
and Carls Winslow but those are just a shows.
These roles are lot more mental than they are tangible.
It aint no accident that so many black men still behave as boys
and can't define fatherhood.
No one ever paved these roads for us.
We are struggling to do it ourselves while still being expected to
carry you on our shoulders.
Sometimes us Kings feel insecure, inadequate and unsure if we
meet the standards of your desires
If we still ignite the flames to your fire.
Compliment us. Remind us that we matter, that you need us and
that we too are full of beauty.
Affection doesn't just begin or end with the width of our arms
around your body but your touch is desired just as much.
Fill us up with your love so we are never half empty.
Some days it feels as if our ribs and back bones are missing
and aint no sunshine when you're gone.
Know that you are and always will be the key
to our peace of mind.
And if there's ever a time that we're quiet, angry, frustrated or
unpredictable know that we are crying on the inside because we too
feel pain. They say crying is like taking your soul to the laundry matt
and we men are well overdue for a cleanse.
Again women, we've been wiping your tears for years.
Today, we need you to wipe ours.

BLACK BOY BLUES

I am afraid for every black boy born.
I am terrified because the moment they're removed from their
mother's womb they are already at war
Already branded X for extinction, expected to be sentenced to
life or death by 25
Orange jump suits and caskets already laid out
for the time they arrive
I've attended more funerals in cemeteries and prison yards than
I've attended high school graduations
Shed enough tears to fill the Nile River
These black boys are drowning in the depths of societies of
rapid waters
Like Katrina victims they are waiting on FEMA to save them
I am afraid for every black boy born.
When my son gets older, our conversations will resemble army
basic training.
I'll tell him, DRESS RIGHT DRESS like you are interviewing
for a job everyday of your life.
Wear your pants on your waist.
Tuck your shirt
And don't dare wear hoodies in unfamiliar places.
FORWARD MARCH!
Walk with purpose like you are determined to reach your
destination. Make sure each step you take is solidified and
synchronized.
Hold your head high where your eyes are visible so your vision
can be shared

ABOUT FACE! When your peers attempt to interrupt your
balance with bashful decisions
make a 180 degree turn around
and reject them from your presence.
Turn your passengers to pedestrians if their presence is not
purposeful for your progression
ATTENTION!
Answer police officers with sir or ma'am.
If they respond with hostility, refrain from raising your voice
and mirroring their ignorance. Don't make sudden moves.
Know that they are looking for reason to harm you
It's something about the beauty of your pigment that makes you
a target for injustice
Why are black boys used as target practice?
Why do black boys often get bombed like 16th street Baptist
churches in Birmingham with no regard for the youthful life inside
their temples?
Why are Tyrone's, Bobbies and Willies lynched daily like
strange fruit by judicial systems in business
with privately owned prisons?
I've yet to receive adequate answers for these questions
so I am afraid for every black boy born.
Afraid they will be burglarized of their youth-filled lives before
they've had the opportunity to step into adulthood.
Afraid that they won't be prepared for the war zone
where they are destined to be causalities due
to color lines of fire.
Afraid that too many wrong places
and wrong times coexist for them.
Afraid they'll become the next Trayvon Martin, Bobby Moore,

Michael Stanley, Emitt Till or Chavis Carter.
I am not prepared to dress their tombstones with rose bushes
I am afraid for every black boy born.
I am afraid that my son will one day let go of my hand
and cross the street on his own.
I'm afraid he won't come home.

WARRIORS

For the 17 year old football jock who was strong enough
to share his poetry with his senior English class.
I hear you. Loud and clear. Let your words be reminders that
even the strongest of warriors sometimes weep in the shadows.
I see you grew tired of hiding, silencing your tongue, running
from your problems like they'd eventually disappear.
I imagine those chain like secrets must've been weighing heavy
on your ankles.
But the day you spoke about it, I watched you emancipate from
the pain like you were finally free from being enslaved.
I watched the burden slide off your back as you stood up erect
and stretched your wings prepared to taste the sky.
Mane you looked like a Tuskeegee airmen the way you used
your wings to beat the odds.
The day you spoke about it, it was no longer your pain alone to
bare. You shattered it like glass to concrete with each stroke of the
pen to pad. Exposed your naked truth in front of the entire class.
Didn't care who laughed. Just knew it had to be done.
It was time to shed new light under the sun and you did it.
Even though you were too small and helpless to lift his selfish
desires and demons off you back then
Now you are stronger and NO your stolen innocence can't be
returned and you may not be able to forgive the illness that caused
a man you once saw as a walking giant to hurt you but at the very
least forgive yourself.
Don't let his demons be the death of you.
Write reminders of your mirror.

"It's not my fault." "Being molested does not make me gay."
"My ugly scars are beautiful." "I define my destiny."
Most importantly, remind yourself you are no longer the victim
but the victor.
Take the pain off repeat and change the music.
You are the DJ to your own emotional party.
Let happiness and joy be your theme song.
Do the wobble with your worries.
Cupid shuffle like the floor is your pain.
Do the NaNa til your tears disappear.
Hit the Quan on your depression.
Electric slide away from misery.
Create an island and isolate yourself before he, misery, start
trying to invite company.
Close your eyes and imagine sand between your toes
soft winds against your skin
calm ocean waters gently bouncing against the shore.
In other words, keep writing until your metaphors
become a place of peace
and the world around you becomes a distant dimension that
don't matter that much.
Let your words be reminders of the day you broke the chains
and became free.

BE-YOU-TI-FUL & BREATHE ON…

ATTEMPTED ROBBERY

As a child, I used to hear kids say cruel things like…..
"Yo hair so nappy, yo mama broke every comb she ever tried to put through it."
"Yo hair so nappy the hair brushes and combs start running when they see you."
"You so black if I turn the lights off I want see nothing but your teeth and eyes."
"You so black that you can cause a solar eclipse. and yo nose. i bet you can smell what the rock is cooking."
"You got them big lips. That's them soup suckers. Black ass. Nappy head ass."

Black children
for the duration of your adolescence be ready for phrases like
this to come at your self-esteem like kamikaze planes on 9/11
but don't be moved.
Stand your ground unlike cowards in Florida but like the citizens of New Orleans.
Even though they may make your tears burst from behind your eye lids like broken levees you won't let them rob you of your culture.
Don't let them take your heritage. Remember Harriet, Sojourner, Malcolm, Mansa Musa, Kunta and Cleopatra.
Your hair may be nappy but remind them that you are a mirror image of Kings and Queens, great leaders and inventors.

Remind them that you are a direct descendent of God and your
skin pigment and hair texture was a mandatory incentive.
Don't let them straighten your curls or untangle your kinks.
Don't let them Michael Jackson your skin tone.
There is nothing wrong with your complexion.
Society is constantly trying to convince you otherwise
but don't let them.
Remind them that your brown brilliance is radiate until their
negative connotations become compliments
Better yet, compliment them until they become uncomfortable
with your kindness.
Until they realize that you are royalty and apologize and begin
begging to put the past behind them.
We all know how folks attitude change when they realize you
are somebody.
Allow them
to worship at your feet.
But don't eat from their kitchens or drink from their glasses.
Know they are aiming for your seat at the end of the table.
Laugh with them even though they found it amusing
to laugh at you.
And I know it's confusing because most of the people laughing
will look just like you.
This is how reverse racism works.
This is what hating yourself looks like.
This is how 400 years of dehumanizing feels.
Black children, there is nothing humorous about hating
your own reflection.
But it's everything to love yourself.

BLACK MAGIC

You sooo black....
that you're MAGIC.
Your black is gold. You're black as coal.
Fuel to fire. I watched you light up the sky.
Midnight black. Stars in your eyes.
Constellations in your mind. Moon in your smile.
You are a galaxy of your own. You give birth to Jupiters and Mars
when you simply lift your tongue and hum... you are mother and
father of music.
Jazz, Hip Hop, Blues, Country, Rock are disciples to you.
You so black.
You black like ink. You spill on pages creating poems with words
that dance to your melodic flow. You so black like scripture in bible.
God speaks in the language of you, black like panther 1966 Huey
and Bobby with black Barrat tilted on your Afro and revolution
tattooed on your heart.
You black like Kunta and Cleopatra, hair nappy.
Never comb out the kinks. No need to fix what ain't broken.
Let them grow until they lock like chains.
Wear your kinks like a crown. You are black like royalty.
Like Nefertiti in Egypt
or like Barack Obama in a White House.
You stand out.
Ain't no missing the mark you make in history.
You blackness is revered and feared, loved and hated.
Duplicated and appropriated by those insufficiently pigmented.
Your blackness is a virtue with value
But it is not for sell.
They pay hundreds of dollars attempting to get closer to your
complexion.
Your melanin is literally worth millions.

Wear your black like Jordan's on your feet and polo on your back. Wear it proud and never for a moment be ashamed.

THEY

August 2016
I was having a conversation with a young lady about children.
It was around 6am on a Sunday morning
at an airport in North Carolina.
I bragged to her about my beautiful 5.
She replies that she has none
but she and her fiance would like to one day.
Assuming, I stated that she and HIM should definitely do it
Creating children is highest form of art.
She replied, "me and THEY eventually would."
Immediately, I was thrown off.
Two things came to mind,
either she doesn't know how to properly use pronouns
or she is in a relationship with multiple people.
She went on to inform me that her fiance whom she referred to
as a THEY was in fact one human with female body parts who was
transitioning to be a gender THEY had most identified with.
Growing up in a culture where heterosexuality was dominant
I was initially appalled that some human found it possible and
somewhat logical to interchange pronouns
to have dual gendership
to coexist as what they were born as and what they aspire to be.
My face expressed cluelessness
and confusion with such a concept.
She went on to explain that THEY were uncomfortable with the
ideal of conforming to either
Most comfortable with just being.

Instead of She-ing or He-ing.
More masculine than feminine.
More male than female. More man than Woman.
I mean who said we all had to be in agreement with Gods
original architecture?
Clearly not THEY because them have decided to reverse the
paint strokes of the greatest artist ever known
Whom is noted to make no mistakes but in this case
has been accused.
Maybe he was creating so many pieces of art
that he misplaced parts.
Maybe his chemist called in sick and the work had to be done so
God mixed the chemicals wrong or right
and that day he was most creative.
Poured more estrogen than testosterone in male anatomies.
More testosterone than estrogen in female anatomies.
Maybe God had a long night and was exhausted from all he
created and was like "you know what, I'm tired. Ima let you
decide."
And then there were THEY's.
Maybe there was an eighth day after God rested.
What if God decided he wanted to do something different.
Maybe these THEYs are the reason for the rainbow
Gods way to celebrate his special mixtures.
I guess that would explain why some say they born this way.
Hell, I don't know but who am I to judge?
Who would I be to tell someone they are NOT.
I can not tell you the blueprint to Gods' plan.
I am merely a man said to be made from sand.
What if all of humanity existed as a THEY?

Nonconforming, coexisting, universal, unconfined,
unrestricted, undefined humans?
Liberated from labels, racists, genders, classes, groups,
pronouns. Who would you be? What would you be?
Or would you simply just BE?

SUICIDE NOTES ON FACEBOOK

"Fuck y'all! So what I'm gay. Yo #MCM in my inbox."
97 Likes and 118 comments
"Fuck this depression. I give up."
53 Likes and 36 comments
"I hate it here."
20 Likes and 7 comments
"My family aint shit."
19 Likes and 3 comments
"I bet y'all miss me when I'm gone."
2 Likes and 18 comments

We, his 3,965 friends watched him kill his self.
We liked it, commented.
Somehow found entertainment is his misery.
Each status, a piece to a complete suicide note.
Literally, murder he wrote.
We read his cries to be saved.
Instead of jumping in, we watched him drown
Anticipating a joke to be revealed
For him to move his feet, wave his arms and swim.
We doubted death while he danced with her on dead sinking soil
with bare feet.
Ready to accept defeat because he had no strength to fight death
on his own.
On repeat he sang a song to remind us he felt alone.
We consoled him with our comments.
I recall hoping he'd find solace in the sympathy of strangers
but I knew that wasn't enough.
On a daily he used his fingers to express himself.
Poured his pain in every post in hopes
his loved ones would hear him
see him, believe him.

Not treat him invisible
Every sign was visible.
Wasn't no hiding the miserable
or the cuts on wrists and ankles.
His family treated his depression like it was a childish scar
and it was
But it was a scar on his heart that had yet to heal nor could he
control it like a car with bald tires on black ice.
He was ill prepared for such a journey.
He wore homo like black skin in KKK parade
afraid, ashamed.
Constant battle with social inferiority and gender identity.
He wanted to live in color in a world that was black and white
Not fully ready to accept his rainbow
Somedays, neither was he.
His insecurities would spread like wild fire.
Burning whoever in his path
Exposing the men in his life who had chosen to hide in the
shadows
I've watched him push men out of closets so that he wouldn't
be an outcast alone.
His actions still didn't change the fact that he was alone
That he was drowning in his own ocean of tears.
He watched suicide on his own watch for the time to STOP....
breathing.
They said he didn't even say goodbye or leave a note saying
Why.
But in actuality he did.
It was written all over his Facebook page.

NAKED

In my dreams

everyone is naked

letting it all hang out

Fully exposed

allowing all their truth to be visible and admired.

No one wears garments of insecurities

accessories of pain, shades of oblivion.

No one hides their scars

Mascaras their imperfections.

In my dreams people are bare

stripped of baggage and burdens.

We all live, breath and exist as our rawest selves.

We all skinny dip in seas of liberation

attempting to wash away the dirt, the hurt

that we've bathed in all our lives.

In my dreams, beauty is not measured by how many pounds you
don't weigh, the length of your legs, size of your breast

the circumference of your booty

but rather the consistency in your character
the purity in your personality
the level of your intellect.

Beauty is not bottled up and bought over the counter.

In my dreams, we do what we want
when we want, where we want, how we want.

We aren't consumed by the ideals and standards society
has for so long confined us with.

In my dreams, we live out loud
in vibrant colors.

We are unapologetically and transparently ourselves
no matter how uncomfortable it may make our neighbors.

In my dreams, no ones tongue is silenced
for the sake of someone else's solace.

We say what we mean with our chest

and with confidence.

We make sure our intentions are crystal clear.

Our thoughts are not prisoners to fear nor the inability to articulate.

In my dreams, our actions aren't motivated
by the opinions of others.

We all set our own trends.

Being yourself is the epitome of cool.

In my dreams you are happy, at peace with the world,
with your enemies, with your violators, with yourself.

You are unbothered, unshackled
from your reasons not to live.

In my dreams, you are everything you ever imagined you could be

Went to all the places you wanted to go

Did all the things you wanted to do.

In my dreams, they all came true.

In my dreams, your dreams are your dreams
and my dreams are my dreams and we never stop
Dreaming.

But most importantly, in my dreams
I am, you are, we are all
naked, liberated

We are all FREE.

CHOOSE HAPPY

SUPER HUMAN

Cars, motorcycles, Skyscrapers, bridges, rockets, airplanes, trains,
computers, cameras, phones, televisions, radios, ultra sound
machines, x rays, elevators, escalators and satellites

All have 1 thing in common.......... They were all created by
these things, these creatures called Humans.
They got 2 hands, 2 feet, 2 eyes, 10 toes, 10 fingers and 1 brain
with 2 sides.
Humans; just like you and me.
Extraordinary beings who created extraordinary things.

Humans; just like you and me.
Their minds erected ideas that gave birth to inventions.

Eager to become the very change in the world they've always
envisioned.
These humans literally took this blank canvas of a life and painted
masterpieces out of passion driven with purpose.

Humans; just like you and me.
My ex, she used to look at things like bridges, the things thousand
pound cars drive across
Air planes, those huge metal things
that literally fly 35,000 feet in the sky
Cameras, those devices that literally freeze and capture moments
in life and every time she says the same thing
"Wow. Somebody thought of that and actually made it happen."

Humans; just like you and me.

A long time ago I decided I wanted people to be wowed

by my existence in this world.
So 4 years ago I quit my $40,000 salary paying job and pursued my
happiness like Christopher Gardner.
I decided to no longer treat my passion
and my purpose like a hobby only suitable for weekends
and vacations.
I decided I no longer wanted to leisurely date my dreams so I said
I do and I will
making a commitment for the rest of my life.

A long time ago I dedicated my life to this dream of mine.
And somedays my dream and I don't along
I say I quit and I'm moving on.
My dream slaps in my face and says shut up
be patient and hold on.
Nothing about this ride is supposed to be easy.

So I straighten up and get back to working daily to lay down the
pavement for my yellow brick road to success.

I no longer desired a normal life so I quit doing the norm.
I instead went from a 9 to 5 building someone else's empire to
working 9 to 9 to build my mine.

It made no sense to keep spending my precious time doing work
that didn't align with my divine direction.

I was tired of complaining to myself;
I hate my job. It's monday again. OMG, my boss gets on my nerves.

I was tired of giving myself excuses.
*I'll take that vacation next year. I mean I really don't need no new car
even though this one barely starts.
I mean going out is for people who aint got no life.*

All the while my life being wasted while slaving for paychecks that
barely got me by.
Now days, I'm hungry. I don't settle for a piece.
I won't the whole dang pie.
I aint reaching for the sky. I don't want a house on a hill.
I want a mansion on jupiter, my address cloud 9.
I want a piece of this world and it will be mine.
I'm reaching for new heights.
No longer settling for Good. I'd much rather be GREAT.
So at night when I go to sleep I am anticipating waking up and
living my dreams
I refuse to be another sun forever eclipsed and forgotten
because I was too afraid to shine.
So cover your eyes and watch me light up this world.

JOURNEY TO SUCCESS

Success stories aren't written overnight.
You add a page each day of your life.
Pencil is not an option in this journal so be mindful of the ink you
pen on these pages.
Mark out the mistakes but keep writing.
Each wrong turn was meant to happen.

God created these curves and bumps in your destiny for a reason.
Your success is a process.
A journey, a road to be traveled.
Expect the flat tires but always be prepared
and keep a spare so you aren't idle for long.
Keep your tank full so you never run out of gas
to support your drive.

You got too far to go to become comfortable onside the road.

Has anyone ever told you you could
that you would
that you're powerful
amazing, intelligent, important?

If not, every day you wake up tell yourself
STARTING NOW, tell yourself
I CAN. I WILL. I AM POWERFUL. I MATTER.
I AM INTELLIGENT. I AM IMPORTANT.

Do not accept NO….. from anyone, not even from yourself.

Again success is not microwavable. It's slow cooked, marinated
and mixed with patience

seasoned with hard work and consistency
served with a cup of perseverance.
So swallow your pride.
Success has no room for hard heads and old dogs not willing
to learn new tricks.

For as long as you live you will always be a student to life.
Take notes and receive the lessons.
Accept them or not,
they are all blessings.

Ask questions but never question your significance.
Know that within you is great power.
Use it wisely and often.

Clip every string attempting to pull at your wings.
Only the best of birds fly with you.
Remove any and all distractions no matter the consequence.
No relationship is worth the sinking of your ship.

Focus on your next step.
Worrying about everything that needs to be done will only
discourage your progression and give birth to procrastination.

Empires are built one brick at a time. Be patient but stay active.
Keep moving your feet. You will eventually get there.

Success is not determined by the amount of cash in your account
but rather by the amount of happiness in your heart.
Don't spend your life chasing what society told you you should be
chasing.
You decide what you want out of this life
so go get it by any means necessary.

You got work to do. And there is no time to be wasting.
Do it now. Don't TRY. Just do it
because TRY aint nothing but a fixation of failure.

LAST TRACK

So that's what I got for y'all.
I hope my words were received.
I hope I impacted you in a positive manner.
I hope that after reading this book of poems that you choose to live
happy and to not allow the world to dictate your choices.
I once read a book called *Art of Living* and in this book it talked
about mastering life.
There was a chapter that stated we should learn the difference
between what we can and what we can't control. We can't control
what we were born into but we can control what we live into, what
we love into. Take control.
The book also talked about how things and situations don't hurt or
harm us but our attitudes towards these things do.
For example, death aint really bad nor the ending of a relationship
but it's our attitudes towards these things that is often negative.
Change your attitude. Choose happy.
If you don't like the definition, change it.
Whatever it is you desire is possible.
You absolutely have the power to make it happen.
You just have to execute on your desires.
There is no shortage of money, opportunity or happiness.
There is just a shortage of people doing
what is required to get their share.
Stop standing on the cliff of life looking at everyone else live and be
happy. Stop sitting around talking and writing on sticky notes about
what you would do if you could do. Stop looking at other peoples
success and being jealous that it aint yours.
Do what they did and jump.
Take a risk.
I promise you
it's worth it.

ABOUT THE AUTHOR

Chris James is a national award winning spoken word poet, TEDx Talks speaker, playwright, educator and published author. In 2016 he was featured on the front cover of Arkansas Times Newspaper for being one of Arkansas' top 20 visionaries. Chris is a member of Foreign Tongues poetry slam team whom ranked 2nd place in the worlds' second largest poetry competition in 2014. He is the founder of Arkansas' premier poetry venue and second black owned art gallery, The House of Art. As a teaching artist, Chris develops and facilitates art integrated poetry writing and performance workshops for K-12 students around the country. He is the creator of stage plays, Dear Black People and The Odds Against U.S.

Chris is the proud father of 5 genius children and the son of Sharon Hardaway.

Book Cover Artwork by Edward Holloway

For Booking or further discussion regarding the body of work
contact us at
PoetrySavesLivesLR@gmail.com

Learn more about Chris James and his Journey @
www.TheChrisJamesJourney.com

Instagram- @ChrisJamesJourney
Facebook- The Chris James Journey

Poetry Audio can be found @
www.TheChrisJamesJourney.bandcamp.com